The Charles Bronson
Book of Poems
'Birdman Opens his Mind' Book One
(The first in a series of Bronson books)

Edited by
Stephen Richards

Illustrations by
Charles Bronson, Esq.

Mirage Publishing
First edition
Published in Great Britain
By Mirage Publishing 1999

A CIP catalogue record for this book
is available from the British Library.

ISBN 1 902578 03 1

Mirage Publishing
PO Box 161
Gateshead
NE8 4WW
Great Britain

Printed and bound in Great Britain by
C P Print Ltd, Swalwell, Newcastle upon Tyne, NE16 3DJ

Cover designed by Printex, Gateshead, NE8 4HX

Contents

SPECIAL THANKS GO TO

Zimmer Magazine, Ian Dury, Graham Kitchen, Sir John Paul Getty, Ksenia, Koestler Awards Trust, Ewan McGreagor for his kind words via his PA Karen McGreagor, James Nicholson, Prison Writing, Inside Time Newspaper, The Prison Reform Trust, The Road to Justice, Maria Williams, Esquire Magazine, The Fatboss Magazine, Paul Ravilious, Ray Gilbert, Fred Low, Mr F Castro; Esq. and a host of other good sports too numerous to mention in this small space, but you know who you all are.

A posthumous thanks to the following

Eamon Collins the author of *Killing Rage* – Stood up to bullying.
(Murdered because of what he stood up against.)
Stanley Kubrick who was considering one of our proposals.
Irfan Hussain – Fellow cartoonist found murdered in India.
Carl Giles Daily Express & Sunday Express Cartoonist – for inspiration

From the President of the Plums/Bronson Mania Club

Charles Arthur Bronson – courted by many, known by few. A truly talented and at the same time, by his own admission, a 'slightly mad genius'. I have only known Charlie for about three years, but the one thing that I have strived to achieve, and taken the flak that went with it, is to give my friend the recognition that he deserves.

I am very glad for him that this book is being published; after all it has taken nearly 26 years to produce!!! Believe me when I tell you that you are lucky to have it in your hands, every ruse going was used by the 'powers that be' to stop Charlie's work reaching you – a wider audience.

Why??? Because here is, allegedly, one of society's blemishes tucked away. Vincent van Gogh cut off his own ear, some artists use stolen human parts in their works – and they get displayed in a big gallery that wins them recognition? Well now I hope you, the reader, will decide that Charlie should be recognised in his own right as a poet, a cartoonist and an artist that has lost the plot. This misunderstood and much maligned human being is being treated like a leper by the very authorities that made him the way he is. Charlie, the stage is yours, give them hell!

"TILL THE END"

Paul Ravilious
(The Black Orchid)

Dedication

To Eira,
My most precious and loved mother
Love you always, Charlie

For those of you in the United Kingdom and other countries that read British newspapers it might not be necessary to introduce Charles Bronson, but for those of you who are from Mars or Venus here then is a brief history of what Charlie, as he likes to be called by his friends, has endured to get this far in life. Our friends in the USA are welcomed and thanks go to Angela Archueleta from New Mexico for her work with USA and British Prisoners.

Out of 26 years served in prison 22 of those years have been in solitary confinement. He is a category 'A' prisoner because of his acts of violence carried out against prison warders. Charlie originally received a seven-year prison sentence for conspiracy to rob, way back then he was known as Mr Michael Peterson, but through a bizarre twist the police knew that he went by the name of Charles Bronson in his unlicensed boxing bouts so, rather tongue in check, that is the name he was charged in nearly 26 years ago in 1974. They say he changed his name in honour of the USA actor who became famous for his role in the *Death Wish* film. This is not so, it was Charlie's boxing manager who picked the name.

Charlie fact file – *Five world records for feats of fitness and strength * Accomplished Chess Grand Master *Won five consecutive Koestler Awards for art, poetry and writing *Did not see the sky for seven years *Can do 132 press ups in 60 seconds *Does 3,500 press ups in his daily workout *Once spat through a cell door flap into the face of child killer Ian Brady *Sent Myra Hindley two packs of cigarettes so she could smoke herself to death *Challenged caged International Assassin Carlos the Jackal to a chess game by post *Achieved his hat trick of Broadmoor rooftop sieges causing over £1 million of damage *Has taken part in 9 roof top sieges *Has taken more hostages than Saddam Hussein, well nearly *Does not smoke or take drugs and feels deeply insulted when asked to undergo prison drug testing *Ran out of bare knuckle opponents when free so took on a 14 stone Rottweiler and won *Minimum of five warders in attendance when Charlie is unlocked *Took three Iraq aeroplane hijackers hostage after they tried to pull him into their cell with the help of five others, they ended up being trussed up and had to tickle Charlie's feet or otherwise! *Has his own fan club *Has his own personalised UK telephone number (0709 11 2766-BRON) *Bored housewives write to him at the rate of a dozen letters a week *Struck up a friendship with a top world class model – Ksenia (The Russian Princess) *Intends opening a chain of restaurants across Europe called 'Bronco's' *Has appeared in just about every magazine and newspaper in the UK that is of any repute *Member of the martial arts organisation World Budo Kai uses Tai Chi *Attained awards for his culinary dishes that he tries out on fellow inmates *Six foot tall weighs a lean 252 pounds.

Charlie has been told from the United Kingdom Home Office via one of their employee's, who I will name and shame in the next book *(Hostage of My Past Vol 1)* unless he withdraws his unwarranted remark, that he will not ever be given: a pre-release home leave, never be granted parole and he will be released straight back into the wild. That was said a matter of weeks before Charlie took his last hostage at Hull prison. Maybe you are just beginning to understand now how the authorities are treating him?

Charlie's father died a few years ago, he was refused permission to attend the funeral. One week before he took his last hostage his grandmother died, permission was refused for him to attend her funeral! Then it was sprung on Charlie that the special unit at Hull prison was closing down and he would be moved to Durham prison, but wait for it... he would have to go back into solitary confinement for a few months until Durham was ready to take him? "Right, Charlie you just go into this holding cell for a few months." And on top of that he was not even told where he would be moved to, just a "Get your kit together you might be moving this week." He had to live out of a box. The staff at Hull had been very good to Charlie, he knew that and respected how they had been fair with him, until Monday 1st February 1999 when Charlie took a civilian worker hostage. Their mind games got to him!

Mirage Publishing had written directly to the Home Secretary; Jack Straw, the Director General of Prisons and the governor of HM Prison Durham, the letters were sent via Recorded Delivery with Advice of Delivery on the morning of the 1st February, Charlie took his hostage in the afternoon. The letters raised concerns at how he was worried over his move and he had turned away from violence using his art as a means of therapy. Jack Straw has not even acknowledged the letter, the Director General gave a brief coverage of how all prisoners would be considered on this and that, waffle....

I personally telephoned the prison immediately on hearing the news on the afternoon of 2nd February offering my services to help end the siege as did Paul Ravilious, Charlie's long standing civilian friend. Did the prison take up our offer of help, you bet they did not! The siege continued until the following day due to the pig headedness of the authorities in thinking they knew best. They had armed officers in the wrecked wing waiting to kill Charlie if the hostage was hurt or worse. They would have been in their element to get rid of this embarrassment to the British Penal system, I was quoted as saying in *The Mirror* newspaper that the hostage would be released unharmed, that is how it ended. Hull prison staff kept their word in allowing Charlie to telephone his solicitor as soon as he gave it up, that is the one saving grace. I feel that the British Government and the Prison Authorities have acted out of hand in this matter. IRA prisoners can go free, Hindley (child killer) can have an army of do gooders argue her case for release, but poor old Charlie (Born 6th December, 1951) must be silenced (of the lamb chop). Would you rather have Charlie back on the streets or Myra Hindley? Why not drop the UK Home Secretary a line at the House of Commons in London, I am sure he would love to hear from you. Charlie loves kids and has an anti-bullying theme for his next Koestler entry. He is running for the vacancy 'Mayor of London' in 2,000 saying that Lord Archer's (also running for the job) idea of putting Scotland two hours behind English time is lunacy. He hates sex offenders saying if they were put in a cell with him then he would make sure that they would not ever be able to re-offend. Could Lord Archer carry out that election promise? Remember that when you vote!

Paul Ravilious was sought out and here in this short space he offers his thoughts. "I'm Chaz's friend the most honourable comparison for people to understand what my friendship is all about is of Pip & Magwich from the novel Great Expectations. I have known Chaz for three years, but in that short space of time we have given each other 'gifts' - experience of life that are unique, fun and exiting. I became a pen pal through the Prison Reform Trust of which I am a member. I have to speak up for Chaz here and let people know that he does a lot of unheralded charity work for Clare House kids hospice in Liverpool, England and has helped me to produce an anti-drug booklet. The roller coaster ride is not over yet.

I wanted to add a few lines to what I have been allowed to write about my dear pal Charlie. The events of early February (hostage) left me feeling angry and sad for him that he had chosen that course of action. It's easy to have sympathy for a friend, but to people who don't know Charlie it's harder to explain his actions. Charlie is now on for move number 54 in the space of only the last two years. He has had hundreds of moves over the years. Moving house is not one of the easiest experiences of what I remember... Moving, death (his father and recently his grandmother) and not being allowed to attend the funeral tipped Charlie over the edge and I believe that Charlie had lost all control of any reasoning ability. He was of diminished responsibility – we as normal civilians find these things hard to cope with – surely prisoners find these trials equally hard as well? Till the end Charlie – Paul."

Thanks for those sentiments Paul; I am sure we can expand on that in the next book. To date Charlie has been slung in a concrete coffin at Whitemoor prison in Cambridgeshire, his art materials have been kept from him, the only object for creating anything he has been allowed to date is a pen, ironically a *Bronson Mania* pen which we used for promotional purposes. He has not even been allowed to telephone anyone. He has not been allowed to read any newspapers or even speak with other prisoners. This is an indictment on the anachronistic penal system in this country, which is as helpful to mental health as a frontal lobotomy. Charlie has mixed with IRA prisoners, serial killers, paedophiles, rapists and real gangsters. Surely the state has to be brought before a court to answer for the treatment it has and still is offering those that are suffering from some form of mental illness. Have you heard the recent suggestions, the UK Government want to bring in a law against those with a personality disorder – imprisonment! Charlie lost the plot years ago, a few little mistakes and wham, bam thank you mam they never forget.

Unfortunately there is not enough space here to go into all the details, but you can be assured Charlie has a story to tell and boy what a story it is. My only fear now is that the prison authorities will continue the ill treatment and mental torture of Charlie as an act of revenge for all of his attacks on prison staff over the years. Any prison officer that carries out these little acts of revenge will be exposed I can promise them that. Just leave Charlie alone to get on with his art and his press ups, he's not harming anyone, until you take what little of his sanity he has left. This is not some Soviet salt mine state, there are laws to protect Charlie as much as there are laws to protect those who Charlie assaults although I firmly believe Charlie was manipulated by the prison authorities and further mentally tortured. I have enough material from my source in the USA to cover another ten books so the authorities are acting in a petty way to stop his art.

Further titles in the Charles Bronson series of books planned for release are as follows:

Hostage of my Past - Vol 1 (Cartoon autobiography of past hostages and full colour violent scenes drawn by Chaz that really will blow your mind)

Hostage of my Past – Vol 2 (Continuation of the above book)

Birdman Blows his Mind (More poems with colour illustrations)

A Mission of Madness (Dare the authorities look inside this one?)

Bronson Rides Again (Boy does he really go to town in this one)

Christmas Cracker Mad Millennium Book (Poetry from Hell) (A real cracker, not a one to forget, a festive feast of madcap madness)

Solitary Fitness (Charlie's secrets of how he managed to get so big, strong and fit, on prison food. Build up strength that will allow you to bend iron bars and punch a hole through bullet-proof glass, just like Charlie did as well as when he punched his way through a steel cell door? No kidding!

All of the above books will be A5 size in hardback full colour or part colour

The Charles Bronson Autobiography with Steve Richards and Paul Ravilious will be something that rattles the cages of everyone in the modern world. This will be the icing on the cake, the daddy of all daddies. The book that will make your ordinary street thug look like Peter Pan. Charlie will be laughing all the way to the crematorium. The self confessed poet from hell and born again cartoonist who has had his head pumped so full of liquid cosh forced into him by the Frankenstein doctors that he says he is now the living dead with a stare of stone, why do you think he wears those shades?

Other Books and products to blow your mind

Join the Charles Bronson fan club receive a certificate of membership, a full colour photograph of Charlie, copies of his certificates of strength feats, a PLUMS (Prison Lunatics, Ugly Mad Society) poster and a questionnaire to confirm that you are qualified enough to receive membership as it is not guaranteed as an automatic right. Interested? For an application form send 2 X UK 1st class stamps or overseas send International Reply Coupons for info to: Plums/Bronson Mania, PO Box 1314, Littlehampton, BN17 5SG, England or telephone the Bronson Hotline and get to speak to someone or listen to a recorded message directly from Charlie: 0709 111 2766 (BRON).

BOOKS BELOW ARE AVAILABLE FROM ALL GOOD BOOK SHOPS IN UK

Viv (Graham) – 'Simply the Best'

True Crime paperback, 242 pages, A5 size ISBN 1-902578-00-7 UK RRP £7.99

New Year's Eve 1993 Viv Graham's life came to a violent end. His involvement with the Geordie Mafia is unfolded. The truth, pain and anguish revealed in this action packed book alongside a gripping catalogue of crime never before compiled. Feared gangland reprisals abruptly end academic views! Newcastle United Director's PA Company refused comments. Spine Chilling real life hitman presently based in Manchester gives his view on the gangland assassination of Viv. Manchester and Newcastle Super City Comparisons. An insight into events that triggered riots across the North East of England. Tyneside and Teesside's criminal underworld explored. An exposé of Ray Mallon, Middlesbrough's suspended CID Chief. North East Murders, Kneecappings, Shootings, Drug Dealing, Protection Rackets, Blackmailing, Robberies, Torturing and more. Microscopic & Graphic details of Viv's murder and funeral. Viv's prophecy of his death. Viv's involvement with Geordie TV star Tim Healey and England soccer player Gazza. Tenerife underworld visits to Tyneside. Gazza writes the foreword.

Viv – and the Geordie Mafia (Vol 2)

The continuation of the above book, 339 pages, A5 size ISBN 1-902578-01-5 UK RRP £9.99

Police seize computer system and disks feigning disinterest in the Viv case. The author and two researchers are arrested for work on another book. Police end up sifting through disks for clues that might help them. The Candy Rock Resort of Blackpool is looked at in detail – drugs & clubs. A convicted beach murderer alleges Viv was his alibi. Clairvoyant Spiritualist contacts Viv's spirit at the Death Site! An exposé of how Roger Cook's team sets up the stooges. More Murders Kneecappings, Shootings, Drug Dealing, Protection Rackets, Blackmailing, Torturing and Scams. Viv's three lovers fight over insurance payouts withheld when his insurers described his death as being self-inflicted! Intimate details from the three women caught in the eternal triangle of love. Love 'em and leave 'em, not likely, they became his possessions. Father Michael Conaty, MBE, speaks about retribution. An original Geordie Mafia member speaks openly and reveals what actually happened when Reggie Kray visited Newcastle, was he really kicked out? Alleged jury-rigging is looked at in detail when alleged pliers torturer Paddy Conroy claims he was convicted on the lies of a co-accused. One of the murder suspects gives first ever interview. Free guide to some of the main nightclubs and pubs on Tyneside, the good, the bad and the ugly. Foreword by John Davison, the North's own World Champ boxer. Was Viv the North's top Drug Baron with a £2m drugs Empire and £40,000 a week income, find out?

PUBLIC *consumer* ENEMY 'The A-Z Handbook of how to complain and win!'

200 pages, 17.8-cm height, paperback handy size ISBN 1-902578-02-3 UK RRP £5.99

Police arrest the author and two researchers for alleged deception. National food and drink companies complain to police about the amount of complaints received! Read how the companies shook with fear when they were put under the microscope by the team of seven tireless titans. Everything tackled from mobile phones, fags, booze, Credit Card Company, electrical suppliers in fact most companies that you would have day to day dealings with. 2,500 companies over an 18-month period are probed with bona fide complaints. You pour out your cornflakes and there it is that burnt black flake. You dig it out and carry on! You put up with it, not this author. The publisher took a drinks company to court, what happened? Read how some companies have been covering up the truth about complaints. Do you eat a Saturday night kebab, after reading this you might not ever touch another one again, Undercover work exposes poor hygiene that could kill. Ralph Nader was the USA Consumer Champ; this man is the UK's.

All of the above titles should be available or can be ordered from good book shops, just give them the ISBN number. Or send cheque/Postal Order (overseas send Int Money order) for the RRP to the Publisher (Address on first page). P+P is free in UK, Europe add 10% rest add 50%

MEN ON POTTIES YOU GOTTA LAUGH
A LIFE OF MADNESS IS THE PATH..
A GOOD OLD CRAP UPON THE CROWN
WAKE IN THE MORNING WITH A FROWN.
PRISON MADNESS AT IT'S BEST
BELIEVE ME NOW IT'S NOT A REST.
TAKE MY ADVISE GIVE PRISON A MISS
IT'S NOT WORTH A BOTTLE OF PISS.
IT'LL DRIVE YOU CRACKERS IT DID WITH ME
THEN THEY THROW AWAY THE KEY.
OH WELL.. LEAVE ME CRAP IN PEACE
GOODNIGHT _ GOD BLESS †

Chris Barr

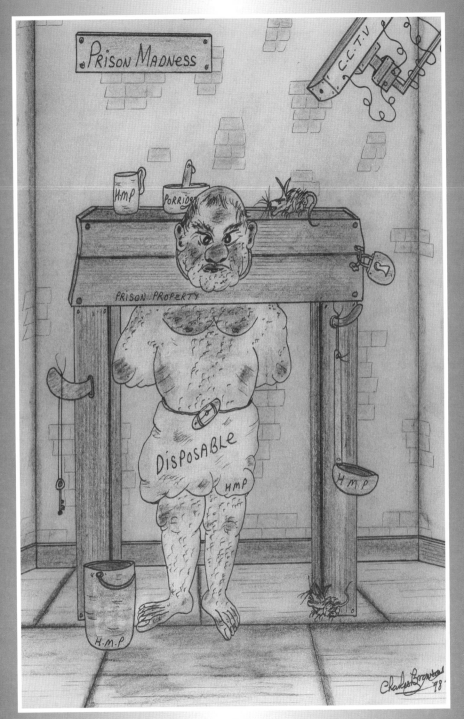

11

The madman's rocking chair

He sat in his old rocking chair thinking of the past
The madness that had ate into his brain
He felt the lobotomy scars and remembered the awesome pain
He began to cry. He began to shake with anger
An egg... it cracks, darkness becomes light, life begins
A journey... a mission of madness

He felt lonely and empty inside
He began to smile, he started to laugh hysterically
He fell off the chair and hit his head on the stone floor

When he awoke he was back in the padded room
All wrapped up in a canvas suit
Life was the asylum
Laughing all the way to the crematorium

Mr Nobody

Knocking, knocking in my head
Not a word is ever said
All that noise in my space
Around your neck an old boot lace
Knock, knock all the time
Go away I'm feeling fine
Can't you see what I am?
You can call me son of Sam
Feel the horns upon my head
Cross me once and you'll be dead
See the sixes on my chest
Now I lay my case to rest

Dedicated to the pratt who shot John Lennon.
I hope you rot in hell you dog!
'You give madmen a bad name!'
I never put your name as you're best forgotten.
You was a nobody and still are a nobody

13

Madness Beyond Belief

Crying – Screaming, echoes from hell
Madmen crawling inside a shell
Damaged brains forever gone
Locked inside denied the sun
Crazy men with broken hearts
Stabbing eyes with rusty darts
Hell on earth in a padded room
Stabbed through the chest with a sharpened broom
Flying eggs inside the brain
Fish with faces it's all insane
A hole in the skull the light shines through
Another lobotomy stuck with glue
Institutionalised beyond repair
A broken telly and they still stare
Psychotropic drugs control the mind
Every madman walking blind
A madman hangs in the early hours
A pauper's grave without flowers
Electric shocks through their head
One too many and then you're dead
Zombied and empty like an old tin can
This is silence of the lamb
Violence erupts it's out of control
A million dreams inside a hole
Forever searching - forever lost
It's your sanity that it costs
Electric eyes with solid steel doors
Sleeping naked on concrete floors
Mental pain creeps through the heart
A reflection of madness from the start
Even the sky is taken away
The son of Sam is out to play
Tears of ice burn your soul
Even the dreams are as black as coal
Never walk backwards into a madman's cell
A laughing lunatic straight from hell

Another leaves in a body bag
Criminally insane was on the tag
Another arrives in a big white van
A raving lunatic, a dangerous man
Broadmoor asylum is the place
Shame and guilt to a human race
A crematorium on top of the hill
Open your mouth and swallow the pill
A madman falls down on his knees
Childhood memories of climbing trees
Another mad-axe man behind the door
He has cut a head off with a saw
A plastic world with padded walls
Pray all you want but no-one calls
A concrete coffin closing in
Wake in the morning in a loony bin
Reaching out but no-one 's there
Finding nits inside your hair
Looking deep inside yourself
A plastic mirror on the shelf
You start to scream. You just can't stop
A gun in your face by a twisted cop
They shoot mad-dogs but cage madmen
I stabbed a guy with a fountain pen
I'm now a hostage of my past
They call me the man in the iron mask
I've had more hostages than Saddam insane
Charlie Bronson is my name

The Crematorium

Saw her sitting outside the crematorium
She kissed a single rose
She crossed herself and walked away
Madness is what she chose
She saw her man go up in flames
The man she never really understood
She walked away with her head up high
To spread the ashes in their favourite wood

IN THE SHADOWS OF MADNESS
THE MAD-MAN SCReAMS...
FACES OF HORROR
INSIDE OF HIS DREAMS!

H.M.P. WOODHILL. MAX-SECURE UNIT

1998

16

A Madman lost his Soul

Dripping blood from a hole in the face
Strangled with an old boot lace
Father time switched out the light
I never got to say goodnight
A size 10 boot crushed my head
My body felt like a lump of lead
Pins and needles in my brain
A bucket of madness dipped in pain
Awaking up in a padded cell
Somebody shouts you're now in hell
Reaching out but no-one's there
You start to pull out chunks of hair
Sucking lemons you never smile
In your throat you feel the bile
A concrete coffin becomes your home
Now your heart it turns to stone
Even your shadow goes away
It's even too late to start to pray
You start to laugh; you loose control
Another madman lost his soul

Misery

Something's blowing in my ear, or am I going mad
I hear a voice inside my head. I believe it is my Dad
Can't seem to escape reality, the past keeps flooding by
Alone in my emptiness I reach up to the sky
There mist be an answer to all this misery
But inside this hell how can an angel see?
Can't you smell the burning, that's my soul on fire
Wrapped around my body is the razor wire
Ice drops fall and pierce your skin
Your hands in chains you cannot win
All around the vultures wait
Now you have become the bait.

17

THE GARDEN OF MADNESS WILL DRIVE YOU INSANE
WATCH A MADMAN RIP OUT HIS BRAIN.
EVEN THE FLOWERS TURN TO BLOOD
ALL THE BODIES IN THE MUD.
BROKEN EGG SHELLS ON THE GROUND
UNDER THE ROCKS SHELLINGTONS FOUND
THE GARDEN OF MADNESS STAY AWAY
MAD-AXE MEN ARE OUT TO PLAY.

ANYONE SEEN THE BIG BAD LOON -- SOMEONE SAID HE'S FLOWN TO THE MOON.
HE'S TAKEN AN EGG AND A BIG SHOT GUN - SOMEONE SAID HE'LL BE BACK SOON.
WHEN HE'S BACK YOUR IN TROUBLE -- HE'LL BLOW YOU AWAY LIKE A BIG FAT BUBBLE ..
THE GARDEN OF MADNESS BURIES YOUR SOUL. THROUGH YOUR HEART A GAPING HOLE.

20

CHAPTER 2

ALL IN A DAYS WORK

22

23

A PRISON OFFICER FOR 30YRS
HE'S SEEN IT ALL. EVEN THE QUEERS.
SUICIDES, STABBINGS. EVEN DEATH
HE'S EVEN TRIED TO GIVE THEM BREATH.
SOME OFFICERS ARE JUST DOING A JOB
WHILE OTHERS KICK YOU IN THE GOB.
SOME I RESPECT SOME I DESPISE
SOME ARE IDIOTS SOME ARE WISE.
BUT THATS LIFE WE ALL HAVE TO SURVIVE
AND I AIM TO STAY ALIVE

Charles Bronson

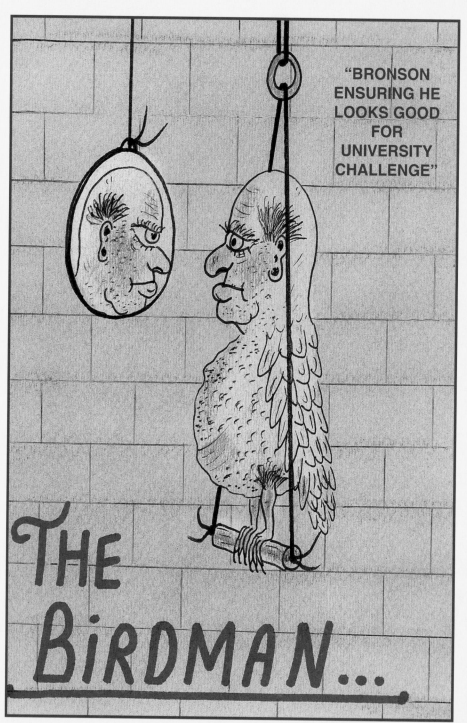

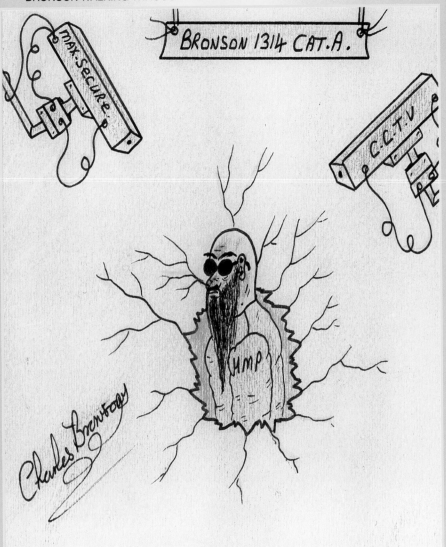

Ian Brady is a pratt
He wants serving with a cricket bat
Myra Hindley is a slag
Choke the bitch with a petrol rag
Old fat West is no good
Chop Rose up for firewood
All the monsters should burn in hell
Or throw the scum down a wishing well

Straffen

John Straffen the monster man
40 years inside the can
He should of hung years ago
He's the original horror show
3 little kids he strangled dead
The devils inside his head
Now an old man waiting to die
The sooner the better, I tell no lie

Ripper

The Yorkshire Ripper lost an eye
What a pity he never died
The guy who done it I'll shake his hand
Bring out the big brass band
Peter Sutcliffe the devil inside
Eyes of Satan you can't hide
Now in Broadmoor until he dies
What a shame it wasn't both eyes

A Message

I've got a message from the firm
Bertie Smalls is a worm
A filthy grass born a rat
He needs serving with a bat
Bertie Smalls the super grass
I'd like to shoot him in the arse

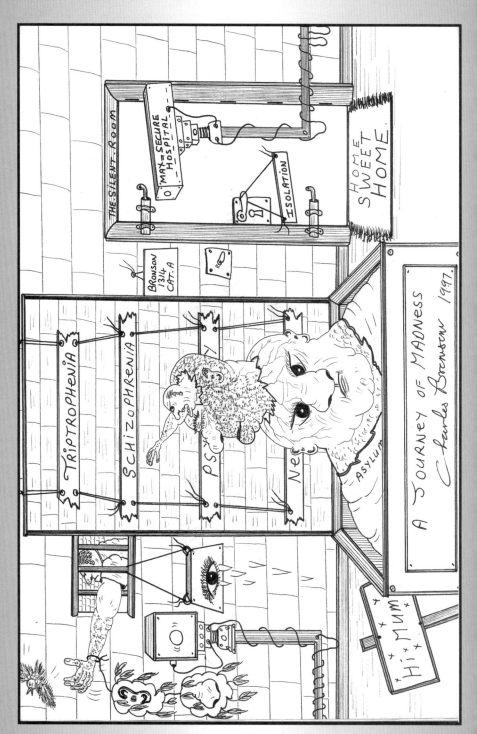

32

"Concrete Coffin"

Charles Bronson.

Like a Tortoise in a Shell
A One way Ride Straight To Hell!
No-more Rainbows in The Sky
Only Darkness until You Die!
Locked Behind A Solid Steel Door
Counting Cockroaches on The Floor!
Eyes That Long To See The Grass
Im The Man in The Iron Mask!
No-way out of A Bottomless Hole
I Feel Ive Almost Lost my Soul!
Im The Birdman with a Broken Wing
The Angels in Hell They Just Cant Sing!
A Damaged Brain with a Broken Dream
Late at Night You'll Hear The Scream!
A Reflection of Madness A Face of Steel
There Are No Tears or Love To Feel!
Lonliness is An Empty Hole
Buried Deep Like A Long Lost Mole!
Nightmares Creep in Through The Wall
Late at Night Satan Call!
No-way out _ No-way In
Forever Lost You Just Cant Win!
The Concrete Coffin A Blanket of Pain
A Big Black Cloud Inside Your Brain!!!!!

Charles Bronson.

1998.

H.M.P. Hull. Special Unit

Concrete Coffin. Concrete Coffin. Concrete Coffin.

33

19.98

Charles Bronson

NIGHTMARES OF A LUNATIC

"INSANITY"

"Licking Honey From A Jar Of Razors"

Charles Bronson

'98'.

PRINTED BY P. RAVILIOUS LTD...

You Gotta Fight it .. Nothing Lasts Forever!
We've all Been There .. it's Never easy.
But There is Hope... "Keep The Faith"
    Believe in Today .. Forget About What Lays-
-Ahead! Coz What Will Be- Will Be.
  it's all Fate.. "Meant To Be"
    So Fight For Today...
  Today is For Living". "Fight it'...... Love it!

INSANITY.

CeRTiFieD MAD.

"Mental Pain"......."Agony"

39

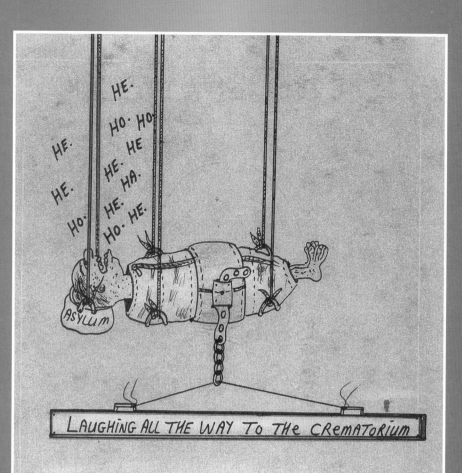

HE WENT TO BED A COMPUTER TECHNICIAN
AND AWOKE A MAD AXE-MAN...
THAT'S HOW INSANE LIFE CAN BE!
ONE DAY YOUR A NORMAL GUY_
_THE NEXT YOUR A RAVING LUNATIC!

"IT COULD BE YOU NEXT"!!

BROADMOOR LUNATIC ASYLUM is
THE DADDY OF ALL ASYLUMS.
IT'S THE HOTEL OF MADNESS.
WHERE MASS KILLERS PLAY POOL
AND PSYCHO'S MAKE FAIRY CAKES.
IT'S THE NEAREST PLACE TO HELL
YOU'LL EVER GET TO.
INSANITY SUCKS OUT YOUR SOUL
AND REPLACES IT WITH PAIN.
IT'S A NIGHTMARE OF A DAMAGED
BRAIN... IT'S A BOTTOMLESS PIT
OF DESPAIR AND MISERY.
    I SPENT FIVE YEARS OF MY
LIFE BEHIND THAT WALL.
    I RIPPED THE ROOF OFF 3 TIMES.
    I STRANGLED A LUNATIC.
    I BECAME A BRICK IN THE WALL
    "UNTIL THEY LOOKED INTO MY
    EYES AND SAW THE TRUTH.
    THEY HAD NO CHOICE BUT TO

MOVE ME BACK TO SANITY —
"I'M THE BIRDMAN"
THEY MUST HAVE THOUGHT I WAS
JUST ANOTHER SNOWMAN MELTING.

        BUT,
THE BIRDMAN DON'T MELT...
"THE CAGE OPENED
"I FLEW"...

        BUT THE MENTAL PAIN GOES ON.
    THERE IS NO ESCAPE FROM MADNESS.
LAUGHING ALL THE WAY TO THE —
    — CREMATORIUM...

                Charles Bronson
                        1999.

41

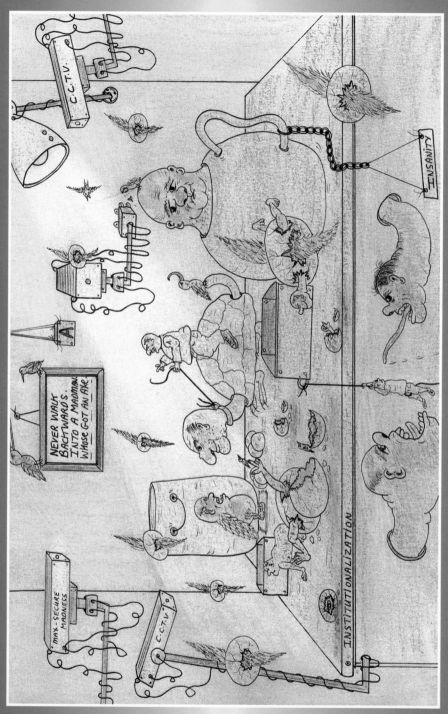

INSANITY.

LABOTOMY STAN
FROM THE ISLE OF MAN.
DOUBLE DANGEROUS
A HOMICIDE MAN.
CERTIFIED MAD FOREVER INSIDE
GOD ONLY KNOWS HOW MANY DIED.

THEY CUT-OUT A PIECE OF HIS BRAIN
THEY SAID HE WAS INSANE.
NOW HE WAKES UP SCREAMING
THEY SAY HE'S ONLY DREAMING.

THEY LOCKED HIM IN A CELL
HE WOKE UP IN A HELL.
NOW HE SITS ALONE
BROADMOOR IS HIS HOME.

HE'S ON PSYCHOTROPIC DRUGS
THEY CAUGHT HIM EATING BUGS.
ANOTHER MADMAN WITHOUT A NAME
HE LIVES HIS LIFE IN PAIN.

THEY GIVE HIM ELECTRIC SHOCKS
HE'S GOT HOLES IN ALL HIS SOCKS.
LABOTOMY LEFT HIM IN A HOLE
NOW HE'S LOST HIS SOUL.

MADNESS IS ONLY A STATE
OF MIND.

IT'S ALL MIND OVER MATTER.
I DON'T MIND —!
AND YOU DON'T MATTER!

LAUGHING ALL THE WAY
TO THE CREMATORIUM!

Charles Bronson

46

47

48

The Cage !

A hole in the ground
There is no sound
A blanket of silence
In a room of gloom
You're a zombie
Forgotten
Beyond touch
Like a hollow tree
Empty
And waiting to die
Even dreams are dark
A big black cloud
The lights gone out
Good night

Poetry

Poetry flows like a stream
Words come like a dream
I'm a poet locked in chains
Poets aim to get in brains
The poet from hell that's me
My poems all run free

Missing

Looking through the bars of shame
I'd love to walk in the rain
The sun no longer shines on me
I'm almost blind t cannot see
I'd love to walk on the grass
Or see some flowers in a vase
Feel the breeze in my face
Even the wind I would race
I wanna swim in the lake
Get my teeth in a fillet steak
Gotta believe in faith and hope
Gotta prove that I can cope!

49

50

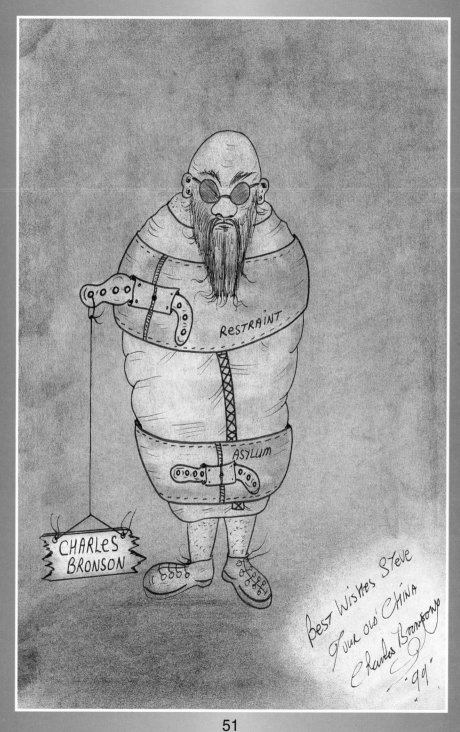

RESTRAINT

ASYLUM

CHARLES
BRONSON

Best Wishes Steve
Your old China
Charles Bronson
'99'

52

We The Willing.
   Lead By The Unknown.
Have Been Doing The Impossible.
   For The Ungrateful.
   For So Long.
   With So Little.

Are We Now
   Qualified
   To Do Anything
      Atall ?...

Never Walk Backwards
Into A Madmans Cage!

Charles Bronson

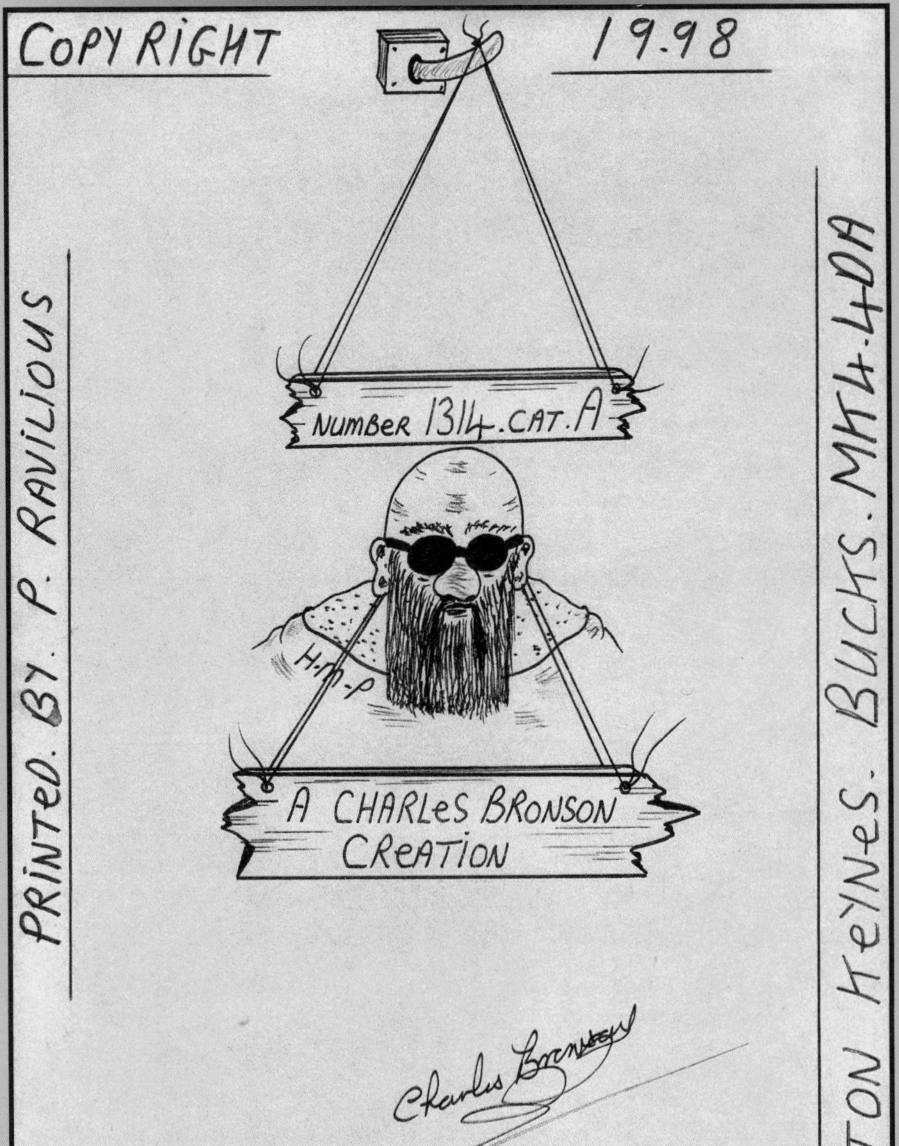
COPY RIGHT
19.98
NUMBER 1314.CAT.A
H.M.P
A CHARLES BRONSON CREATION
PRINTED. BY. P. RAVILIOUS
MILTON KEYNES. BUCKS. MK4.4DA
Charles Bronson
H.M.P. WOODHILL_MAX-SECURE UNIT.

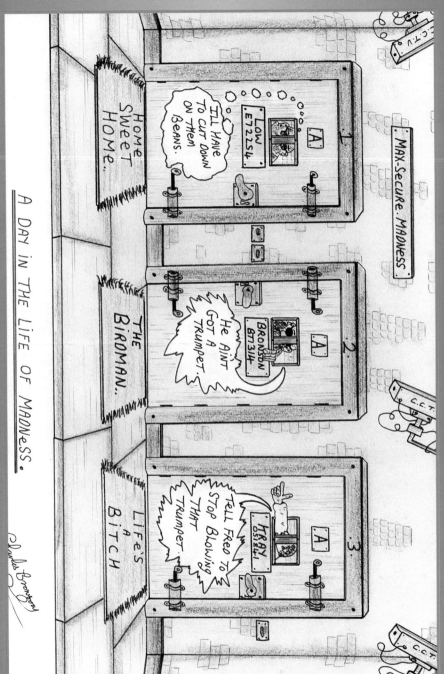

Spider

Life's a bitch!
It's never easy when you lose a friend
But I done my best to give it a good send off!
A match box, 30 match heads and up it went
A good crematorium
Now Fred's gotta get on with life
Well four lives for Fred
Word as it...he's got a little baby spider

Madmen and more madmen

In the day of a life of a madman
Unless your mad how can you know?
He lives in a world of his own
Much like a one-man show
Never intrude on a madman
Unless you've an apple pie
Or you could end up victim
Without a pie you'll probably die!!

Madmen are sensitive and emotional
They laugh where others cry
So laugh along with a madman
Always best to pacify
If they're tired let them sleep
Tuck them up with a nice fur rug
And when they awake in the morning
They like chocolate in their mug!!

Most madmen love the planet
It's the people that they hate
They like to cuddle animals
A spider is their best mate
Most madmen love to sing
Some they sing and dance
When they have a sing-song
Best you stay away

57

58

Viv Graham

Viv Graham Simply the Best
In peace the man now rest
Memories he left us all
Great guys they have to fall
Viv was a man until the end
Just my respect is all I send

The Twins

Ronnie and Reggie men of steel
I'm honoured to have shared a meal
No longer with us Ronnie Kray
At his funeral they played my way
Ronnie Kray was my best friend
A solid man who never pretended
I loved him like my dad
Respect is what he had
I met the Twins in Parkhurst jail
I stabbed a nonce with a six-inch nail
Me and Ron went to Broadmoor
Madness is what we saw
Crazy years but what the hell
A cell is just a cell
After 30 years Reg is still inside
His Mum and Dad and Ron have died
For god sake let him free
The Twins mean a lot to me!
It's madness right to the core
Poor Reg is behind the door!

Joe Pyle

Joe Pyle's a man of honour
And solid friend to me
Not many left of his breed
A born king indeed

The Rainbow

Chasing a rainbow across a sheet of glass
Living inside this iron mask
Catching a rat inside your bed
Go to sleep and pray you're dead
Watching a spider spin a web
Sitting alone on the ebb
Smelling death in the air
Why do dead men always stare?
Touching the wings of a lady bird
A madman's cries are never heard

'Dedicated to mad Frankie'

Biggsy

Ronnie Biggs is the best
He escaped in a prison vest
Good old Ronnie made the grade
The great train robbery what a raid
Now on his toes for 30 years
A Brazilian beach with a few beers
3 cheers for Ronnie hip hip hooray
And they say crime doesn't pay

Bob Mawdsley

The real life Hannibal is my mate
Call him a nutter he'll punch you in the gob
He killed two cons in Wakefield hick
Paedophiles they make him sick
Now in a cage for twenty years
He sleeps in peace he has no fears
Bobs alright he's my friend
My best wishes I do send

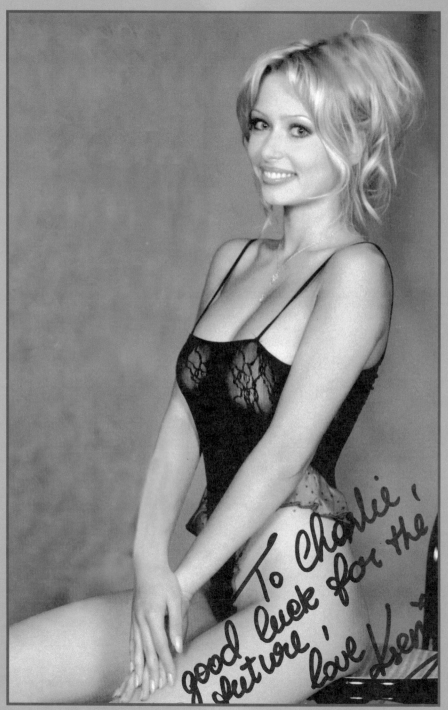

To Charlie,
good luck for the
future,
love Kent

62

PRISON = MADNESS.

WALKING ON BROKEN GLASS
EATING RAZOR BLADES.
RIPPING CHUNKS OF MEAT OFF
BLEEDING IN A WELL
THE WORLD'S GONE MAD.
STOP THE BUS AND LET ME OFF!
A BLIND MAN IN A SAUNA
EATING APPLE PIES.
NO LOVE IN A BOTTOMLESS HOLE
THE RIPPER RIPPED HIS SOUL.
A CAVEMAN IN A TENT
EATING WORMS WITH CHIPS
THE WORLD'S GONE MAD
SOMEBODY PUT A HOLE IN MY NUT

FULL STOP

IT'S 1999 AND IM IN A HOLE
I SENSE IV'E LOST MY SOUL!
YEARS ARE FLYING BYE.
TWENTY FIVE I TELL NO LIE.
A QUARTER OF A CENTURY BEHIND THE WALL
A PLACE WHERE NO ANGEL'S CALL.
FOREVER IN SPACE NOTHING THERE
A LIFE OF HELL WHERE NO-ONE CARE.
1999 HERE WE GO
EYES ON FIRE THE HEARTS A GLOW!

66

I Went To Sleep An Angel
I Awoke In-side A Cage.
I Walked Across A Field
I Fell Inside A Hole.
I Once Had A Smile Of Gold
Now My Face Is Stone...

I'm The Birdman Without A Soul
My Dreams Are Black As Coal.
I'm Empty Like A Shell
My World Is Just A Hell.
I'm The Man Without A Heart
My Hope Was Torn Apart.
I'm The One They Call The Loon
My Face Is In The Moon.

Roses Are Red So Is Blood
I'll Bury Your Head In The Mud.
Love Is The Destruction Of Man
It's The Silence Of The Lamb.

I'm In Love With An Apple Pie
I'll Stab You Through The Eye.
The World's Gone Insane
Lets Eat A Monkey's Brain.
Ba. Ba. Black Sheep In The Abottoir
Cut It's Throat With Cheese Wire.
Lets Blow Off Santas Head
And Put A Tart In My Bed

I've Eat More Porridge Than Goldilox
All I Do Is Smash Up Rocks...
I've Had More Hostages Than Saddam Insane
Charlie Bronson Is My Name.
25 Yrs Behind This Door
I Sleep Alone On A Concrete Floor.
Many Say I'll Rot Inside
But When I Go. I'll Go With Pride.'
Yeh Im The Poet. Im The One.
Melt Your Face In The Sun
Go Such A Razor Blade. Yeh!

A Reflection of Madness.

Like a Blow to the Skull - A massive Hole
in the Face. Ripped and Bleeding in the
Chains of Shame - Crippled with emotions -
A madman screams the ultimate nightmare.
Walking back into the Padded Room - into the
Stench of Insanity - into the Darkest Room.
A Body wrapped in canvas - Empty and alone -
Soul torn and smashed -
Smashed into Adversity by the Hand of Steel.

Look into the Mirror of the Mind and
Go Deep within Yourself
Blow away the Shadows of Fear
Rip out the Nightmares of Life
The Reflection is madness
Your as Mad as the March Hare
Your the Maddest of them all...

Free Your Mind of Pain
Open up Your Brain.

The Birdman of Broadmoor.

The Birdman's Got a Broken Heart
Madness Ripped His World Apart.
Certified Insane and in a Cage
Trapped Inside and Full of Rage.
The Birdman says He Dont Care
Eyes of Marble. Always Stare.
The Birdmans Got a Face of Stone
Now the Asylum is His Home.

No Sky - No Grass - No Flowers or Trees
A Hopeless Man on His Knees.
No Tears. No Laughter. No Sense of Touch
Even Dreams Dont Come to Much.
The Birdman's Forgot How to Fly
Walking Dead they Do Not Die

Laughing all the way to the Silent Room.
Screams are Silent.
Why Bother?
Charles Bronson

68

MADNESS BREEDS INSIDE THE BRAIN
YOU GO TO SLEEP AND AWAKE INSANE.
ALL AROUND MADMEN LAUGH
I STRANGLED GRANDPA IN THE BATH.
BROADMOOR ASYLUM IS THE BEST
I SHOT A MONSTER IN THE CHEST.
NIGHTMARES OF A DAMAGED BRAIN
THEY FOUND A BODY IN THE DRAIN.
LIVING INSIDE A BOTTOMLESS HOLE
ONCE IN BROADMOOR YOU LOSE YOUR SOUL.
FOREVER LOST - FOREVER GONE
A LIVING DEATH BECOMES THE SONG.
MADNESS FLOWS LIKE A STREAM
EVERY NIGHT YOU START TO SCREAM.
BORN AGAIN - YOUR BORN IN HELL
AN IRON CAGE BECOMES YOUR SHELL.
A SILENT SCREAM DEEP WITHIN
SATAN RIPS YOU LIMB FROM LIMB.
A CONCRETE COFFIN INSIDE YOUR HEART
BROADMOOR RIPS YOUR WORLD APART.
HOW MUCH MORE CAN WE TAKE
THEY FOUND A BODY IN THE LAKE.
IT'S NINETY NINE A BRAND NEW YEAR
A MAN OF STEEL AS NO FEAR.

THE BIRDMAN'S GOT A BROKEN HEART
THIS STINKING PLANET BROKE HIM APART.
IN AND OUT OF A CANVAS SUIT
IN HIS FACE A SIZE TEN BOOT.
THE BIRDMAN'S GOT A FACE OF STONE
NOW THE ASYLUM IS HIS HOME
THE ASYLUM WALL TOUCHES THE SKY
BORN INSANE UNTIL YOU DIE..

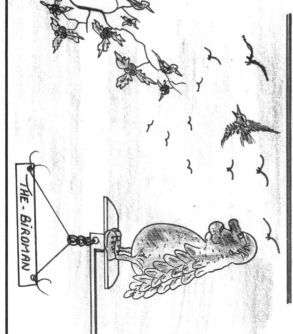

THE · BIRDMAN

IN THE BLACKEST HOLE. SILENCE SLEEPS
ONLY BLINDNESS EVER WEEPS.
TEARS OF ICE BURN THE SKIN
HELL ON EARTH THE ULTIMATE SIN
THE SILENT SCREAM IS IN YOUR HEAD
FACE REALITY YOU'RE REALLY DEAD.
NO-WAY OUT OF SATANS HOLE
THE SON OF LUCY STOLE YOUR SOUL.
ALL ALONE WITHOUT A SKY
YOU NEVER GOT TO SAY GOODBYE -
THE INSANE LAUGHTER IN YOUR MIND
MENTAL PAIN IS ALL YOU'LL FIND.
LIVING ON A RAZORS EDGE
REVENGE IS THE ONLY PLEDGE
THE SILENT SCREAM FOREVER MORE
IN YOUR FACE A SOLID DOOR
A FACE OF STONE CRACKED AND WARN
GOD YOU HATE THE DAY YOUR BORN.

THE SILENT SCREAM IS SOMETHING ONLY THE
ONE'S IN SOLITARY WILL UNDERSTAND.

IT EATS INTO A MAN.
IT RIPS OUT HIS INSIDES
IT CHANGES A GUY.   YOU BECOME MORE
LET ME EXPLAIN - - -   YOU BECOME MORE
ANIMAL THAN HUMAN - YOUR INSANE.

YOU HAVE TO BE CRAZY TO SURVIVE IT.

"ME" - - I LOST THE PLOT YEARS AGO.
I'M NOW MORE IN LOVE WITH FOOD THAN PEOPLE.
FOOD SMELLS AND TASTES BETTER
IT LOOKS NICE TO.
IT KEEPS ME ALIVE.

"PEOPLE" - - THEY BLEED YOU DRY - DO YOU IN THE BACK.
MAYBE I SHOULD EAT THEM?

THE SILENT SCREAM IS THE ULTIMATE TEST
TO A MANS CHARACTER.

I DONT SUGGEST YOU TRY IT...
BUT IF IT EVER COMES YOUR WAY - YOU MUST
GRAB IT WITH BOTH HANDS AND CHOKE IT TO DEATH.

IN THE NAME OF MADNESS

Charles Bronson
7.1.99

PS. ITS NOT THE SCREAM THAT WILL KILL YOU.
"IT'S THE SILENCE"

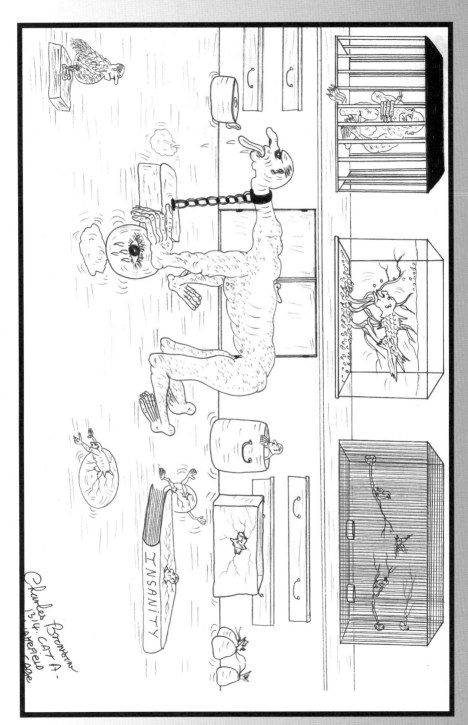

71

BRITISH

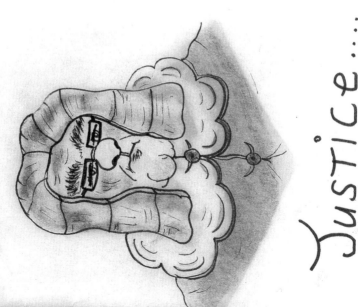

JUSTICE....

THE OLD BAILEY STANDS
IN A SHADOW OF SHAME.
BRITISH JUSTICE
IS FULL OF PAIN.
THE BIRMINGHAM 6
THE GUILFORD 4.
PAIN AND GRIEF BEHIND A DOOR.
HOW MANY INNOCENT MEN?
WERE CONDEMED TO DEATH.
HOW MANY SOULS
RUN OUT OF BREATH.
BRITISH JUSTICE
HISS MY A*** !!!

THE BIRDMAN'S GOT A FACE OF STONE
MAX-SECURE IS HIS HOME
A BROKEN HEART WITH A DAMAGED BRAIN
LOST AND EMPTY AND INSANE.
THE BIRDMAN'S GOT A BROKEN WING
ANGELS OF HELL NEVER SING
HE SITS ALONE IN A ROCKING CHAIR
EYES OF MARBLE ONLY STARE.
THE BIRDMAN'S NEVER GONNA FLY NO-MORE
HE SLEEPS ALONE ON A CONCRETE FLOOR.
FOREVER DREAMING OF THE PAST
HE'S THE ONE IN THE IRON MASK.
THE BIRDMAN ATE MORE PORRIDGE THAN THE 3 BEARS
ONCE IN BROADMOOR NO-ONE CARES.
IN AND OUT OF A CANVAS SUIT
IN HIS FACE A SIZE '10' BOOT.
THE BIRDMAN'S NEVER GONNA SEE THE SKY
TEARS OF BLOOD DRIP FROM HIS EYE
A PADDED ROOM INSIDE HIS MIND
A LONG LOST SOUL SO HARD TO FIND.
THE BIRDMAN'S LIVING INSIDE A SHELL
THIS IS THE LIFE STRAIGHT TO HELL
A ONE WAY TICKET - NO-WAY BACK
THEY TAKE YOU OUT IN A SACK.

THE BIRDMAN IS THE KING OF RAP
HE NEVER TAKES ANY CRAP.
MARK MORRISSON IS A PRATT
GARY GLITTER IS A RAT.
HE WRITES HIS SONGS IN A CELL
RAP SONGS STRAIGHT FROM HELL.
ELVIS WAS A SACK OF SHIT
I'M THE GUY WHO SUCKED DOLLIES TIT
THE BIRDMAN SAYS KEEP IT SWEET
LET OLD FERGIE LICK YOUR FEET
THE SON OF SAM WAS A BROTHER
MY AUNTY ELSIE WAS HIS MOTHER......

ROSES ARE RED SO IS BLOOD
I BURIED GRANDPOP IN THE MUD.
MUMMY HIT ME WITH A HAMMER
THEY BANGED HER UP IN THE SLAMMER
DADDY JUMPED INTO A TRAIN
IN A PICKLED JAR THEY PUT HIS BRAIN.
LIFES A BITCH SO WAS NANNY
SHE HAD A TUNNEL FOR A FANNY

The Bitter Judge

The old bitter judge stared at me
I read his mind what he thought of me
Those words he spoke are in my head
There'll be with me until I'm dead
"You are Britain's most dangerous man"
The living silence of the lamb
You're going to prison for a very long time
Madness was your only crime
You should be in Broadmoor with the insane
Is Charles Bronson really your name?
No your honour that's not my name
And I'll tell you I'm not insane
I'm just a hostage of my past
Having fun time goes fast
I'll bounce back have no fear
Crack on your honour I'll have a beer

Crazy Prison Rules

I closed my eyes and prayed they would never open again
What good is a writer without a pen?
How can you create in a darken cell
I'm on a slow boat straight to hell
Now I'm weak they've stole my gift
Like a rat it's in real swift
The artist is no more
Everything ends behind this door
I needed so much to create
But they fill me with so much hate
It feels like my fingers are gone
Just a black hole where a light once shone
Sure I'm mad I don't deny
But without my art... I'd sooner die

*In protest to Charles having his art taken away
he started a hunger strike!*

74

MISSION OF MADNESS

75

There is ALWAYS A LIGHT
There is ALWAYS Hope.
BUT THERE'S NEVER ENOUGH TIME

Charles Bronson